This engraving of the Great Bridge appeared as a picture postcard issued by Edwin
1920s. It was taken from a design used last century on cheques of the Wilts and

FORDINGBRIDGE
AND DISTRICT
A Pictorial History

This photograph is extremely evocative of the life of the ordinary cottager around the turn of the century. Similar large vegetable patches could be seen in every garden of the time. This row of 17th-century cottages is thought to have been at Outwick—a group here was destroyed by fire, soon after the date of this photograph. The cottages were never rebuilt and the site is now incorporated into the edge of a large arable field.

FORDINGBRIDGE AND DISTRICT
A Pictorial History

Anthony Light and Gerald Ponting

Phillimore

1994

Published by
PHILLIMORE & CO. LTD.,
Shopwyke Manor Barn, Chichester, West Sussex

© Anthony Light and Gerald Ponting, 1994

ISBN 0 85033 897 2

Printed and bound in Great Britain by
BIDDLES LTD.
Guildford, Surrey

List of Illustrations

Frontispiece: Outwick, *c.*1895

Fordingbridge Street Scenes
1. Church Square, *c.*1890
2. The Quadrant Almshouses, *c.*1910
3. Woman and child, Brook Terrace, *c.*1910
4. Knowles Bridge, *c.*1925
5. Town Mill, *c.*1905
6. Provost Street, *c.*1895
7. Provost Street, snow storm, 1908
8. The Market Place, *c.*1920
9. Shaftesbury Street, *c.*1895
10. High Street, *c.*1910
11. Bank Corner, *c.*1910
12. Riverside tea gardens, *c.*1930
13. Horseport, *c.*1895
14. Horseport, *c.*1905
15. Salisbury Street, *c.*1895
16. The Old Manor House, *c.*1895
17. South Lodge, *c.*1895

Forest-edge Villages
18. Blissford Hill, *c.*1895
19. Hyde, 1905
20. Woodman's cottage, Hyde, *c.*1900
21. Woodgreen murals, 1933
22. Riverside camp, Sandy Balls, *c.*1930
23. The folkmoot, Sandy Balls, 1926
24. Castle Hill, Woodgreen, *c.*1910

Valley Villages
25. Yew Tree Farm, Breamore, *c.*1900
26. Well Cottage, Breamore, *c.*1895
27. The Lodge, Breamore, *c.*1905
28. Breamore stocks, *c.*1900
29. Outwick Street, *c.*1895
30. Burgate Cross, *c.*1930
31. North Lodge, Burgate, *c.*1895
32. Avonside, *c.*1930
33. East Mill, *c.*1930
34. Bickton Mill, *c.*1900

Downland Villages
35. The Whitsbury road, *c.*1905
36. Whitsbury Street, *c.*1910
37. Rockbourne, *c.*1910
38. Rockbourne Street, winter, *c.*1895
39. Rockbourne Street, summer, *c.*1895
40. Damerham, South End, *c.*1900
41. Damerham, Mill End, *c.*1900
42. Bridge Street, Damerham, *c.*1910
43. 'Woodview', Damerham, *c.*1910
44. Martin Cross, *c.*1905
45. College House, Martin, *c.*1900

Schools and Churches
46. Harbridge School, *c.*1895
47. Fordingbridge Girls' class, *c.*1908
48. Martin School, *c.*1910
49. Godshill Sunday School outing, 1914
50. Godshill School, 1924
51. Fordingbridge School, 1930
52. Breamore School, 1947
53. Fordingbridge church, *c.*1900
54. Fordingbridge church, *c.*1925
55. Congregational chapel, Fordingbridge, *c.*1905
56. Breamore church, *c.*1895
57. Rockbourne manorial chapel, *c.*1910
58. Hyde church, *c.*1905
59. Bustard Farm, Martin, *c.*1905
60. Roman Catholic church, Martin, *c.*1902

Special Days
61. Gillian Quertier's wedding, 1901
62. Nursery rhyme characters, *c.*1902
63. Mr. McArdle's monoplane, 1910
64. Coronation, 1911, Shaftesbury Street
65. Coronation, 1911, Church Square
66. Coronation, 1911, High Street
67. Coronation, 1911, Clowns' Band

Acknowledgements

Collecting the material for this book has been a fascinating process, made all the more pleasurable by the willingness of everyone we approached to lend their treasured old photos and to delve into their memories for help with the captions.

Mr. John Shering's help and assistance have been invaluable; compiling this book would have been impossible without the loan of many photographs from the Shering Museum, Church Square, Fordingbridge—by far our largest source of material: 3, 7, 35, 43, 44, 47, 51, 62, 64-8, 70, 72, 74, 76-90, 92-4, 96-8, 100, 101, 103, 104, 108-14, 121-4, 126-41, 143-9, 153, 155, 170.

The late Phillip Allison's collection was loaned to us by his widow, Mrs. Lesley Allison. It included no. 167 and the postcard of the murals in Woodgreen Village Hall (no. 21), originally published by M. S. Brewer of Woodgreen. The most valuable part of the collection, however, were the superb prints prepared for Mr. Allison from James Coventry's original glass negatives. Both negatives and prints are now in the care of the Hampshire Record Office in Winchester (reference numbers 33M84 and 105M93 respectively): frontis- piece, 1, 6, 9, 13, 15-18, 20, 25, 26, 28, 29, 31, 34, 38-41, 45, 46, 56, 107, 158-62, 164.

Mrs. J. Cormack loaned us a number of photographs from the Westlake family collec- tion: 22, 23, 49, 50, 61, 105, 154, 156, 157.

Other individuals loaning photographs were: E. Bacon, 118, 120; Mrs. K. Bacon, 19, 63, 102, 106; L. Bailey, 125, 172, 173; E. Hulse, Esq., 165; Mrs. N. Nanson, 69, 151; Mrs. D. Welfare, 48, 59, 60; J. Wort, 117, 119, 174.

The following photographs are in the possession of the authors or their families: Anthony Light: 2, 4, 5, 8, 10-12, 14, 24, 27, 30, 32, 33, 36, 37, 42, 53-5, 57, 58, 71, 115, 116, 142, 150, 152, 163, 166, 168, 169, 171, 177; Gerald Ponting: 52, 73, 75, 95, 99, 101, 175, 176, 178-81.

Among the photographs listed above, four were taken by photographers for local newspapers and we thank the *Bournemouth Times* for permission to use no. 180 and the *Salisbury Journal* for numbers 73, 74 and 106.

All of those who loaned photographs also helped with information for captions, as did Mrs. E. A. Ponting and Mr. E. W. Trim, both of Breamore. Thanks are also due to other members of our families and particularly to our wives for all their interest and support during the preparation of this book.

Fordingbridge almanacs and directories of various dates were invaluable sources of information, particularly on shop-keepers and other traders. Though now long out-of-print, we must also acknowledge a debt to A. T. Morley Hewitt's book, *The Story of Fordingbridge in Fact and Fancy* (privately published in 1966).

We have tried to be as accurate as possible in all our captions, but unintentional errors may have crept in. We would be very pleased to hear from anyone who has further information on any of the photographs included—or who has additional photographs which might be suitable for future publication.

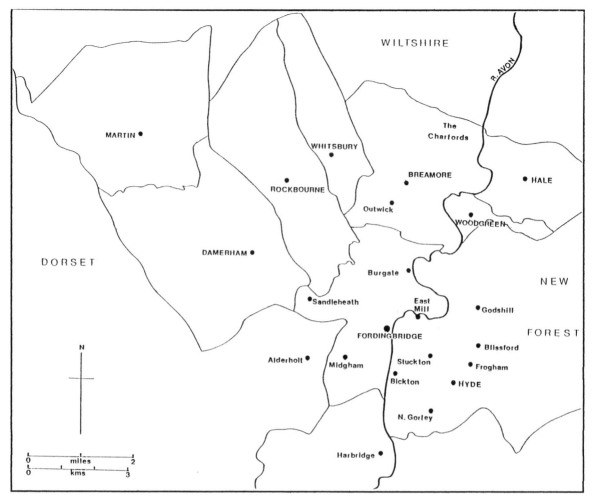

Fordingbridge District, showing parishes.

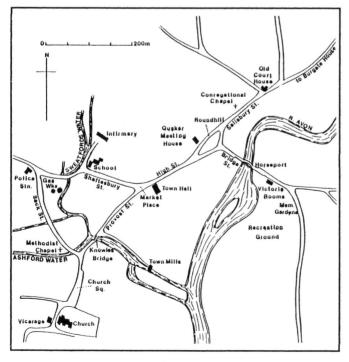

The town of Fordingbridge as it appeared in the early part of the 20th century.

Introduction

Look at a county map of southern England and you will see a 'finger' of Hampshire projecting into Wiltshire and Dorset. At the base of this finger and right on the edge of the New Forest is the small town of Fordingbridge. Formerly a market town and centre of a medieval hundred, and always an important crossing point of the River Avon, the town is still a focus for the surrounding villages.

Fordingbridge lies in the rich and fertile valley of the River Avon, slightly less than halfway from Salisbury to the river's mouth at Christchurch. The villages of Breamore and Burgate also lie within the valley, with extensive areas of meadow in the flood-plain. The valley floor slopes up to the west, where gravels and silts have long provided good quality arable land. Further up the slopes are clay deposits, which have been widely exploited for brick-making, notably at Sandleheath and Outwick. The clay soils also support areas of woodland, very important in the village economies in the past, both for animals to browse and as a source of timber used for building, fencing and many other purposes. A third, much smaller village, Bickton, situated in the narrower section of the valley to the south of Fordingbridge, has always been dominated by its mill. Today, the mill has been converted to maisonettes, and water from the river diverted to form a trout farm, popular with locals and visitors alike.

West again, beyond the wooded clay slopes, the ground rises to chalk downland—the eastern edge of Cranborne Chase. In this area grew up the large and prosperous villages of Rockbourne and Damerham, nestling in the valleys of fickle chalk streams, tributaries of the Avon. Further up the Allen valley from Damerham is the once-remote village of Martin, famous from W. H. Hudson's *A Shepherd's Life*. Between Rockbourne and Breamore lies the village of Whitsbury—historically always a small settlement. Perhaps it did not grow larger because, unusually, it lacks a stream or any obvious source of water. To the Hampshire planners based in Winchester, these chalkland villages beyond the Avon valley, the fringes of the county, are today collectively known as the 'Western Downland'. For centuries, the downs were open grazing for multitudes of sheep; today most of the sheep have gone, the land has been converted to arable, and corn is the predominant crop. Expanses of true downland turf with its unique flora and fauna are now few and far between, Martin Down National Nature Reserve being the largest and best example. (Martin, Whitsbury and Damerham were all part of Wiltshire till 1895.)

To the east of the Avon valley is an area which is very different, geologically, ecologically and in its traditional life-style. The acid heathlands and woodlands of the New Forest form a marked contrast, even today, to the rolling chalk downland. The 'forest-edge' villages and hamlets of, from north to south, Hale, Woodgreen, Godshill, Blissford, Stuckton, Frogham, Hyde, Hungerford, Ogdens, and North Gorley are all situated on gravel terraces, where the land rises from the river valley towards the Forest proper. While not all of these settlements have always been within the recognised boundaries of the New Forest, their lands and people have always been tied closely to it. Tenants of smallholdings here are generally still commoners of the Forest and indeed, even in the valley villages, many tenants have, for centuries, enjoyed common grazing and other forest rights.

From earliest times, man has inhabited the area. On the chalk downlands, earthworks of the Neolithic (New Stone Age) and of the Bronze Age are still to be seen. Continuing archaeological investigation is uncovering less obvious evidence for habitation, such as flint tools and pottery sherds. From this evidence, it is clear that these prehistoric people lived, not just on the downs, but in all parts of the region. By the Iron Age (c.800 B.C.-A.D. 43), farms and villages were becoming as densely spread in the landscape as they were to be in medieval times. Large defensive earthworks exist from this period at Frankenbury near Godshill and at Castle Ditches in Whitsbury. Neither of these has seen large-scale excavation, but from the evidence of Danebury (near Stockbridge), it is probable that each was an important administrative and economic centre for the surrounding countryside—as well as a refuge for local farmers and their families in troubled times.

The Roman invasion of A.D. 43, against which hill-forts offered only short-lived defence, probably did little to alter the pattern of farming and settlement already established in the area. There can be little doubt, though, that over the four centuries of Roman influence, material standards of living improved considerably, even for the most humble inhabitants of farms and villages. The most important and well-known settlement in this area was the extensive Roman villa at Rockbourne, excavated between 1956 and 1974 by the late A. T. Morley Hewitt and cared for today by the Hampshire County Museums Service. This was no doubt the equivalent of a great country house in later times and the centre of a large farming estate; perhaps it was deliberately sited not far from Whitsbury to replace the influence of whatever chieftain had resided at Castle Ditches. Less obvious Romano-British settlements have also been identified by archaeologists not only in the Avon Valley, but also on the gravel terraces and on the chalk downlands.

Inevitably, we have little knowledge of the area from the Dark Ages which followed the departure of the Roman legions in A.D. 410, although archaeological evidence suggests that some farms at Breamore and at Bickton continued in use at this time. One event of national significance took place in c.500 (some sources say 519) at Charford, just north of Breamore. A Saxon invasion force led by Cerdic had landed, perhaps on the shores of Southampton Water, and was advancing westward. The native British forces attempted to stop the advance at the river, but were defeated at the 'Battle of Cerdic's Ford'. (The name Charford is believed to derive from Cerdic's Ford.) Cerdic became king in this area, founding the West Saxon dynasty, an event which was recorded in the Anglo-Saxon Chronicle with the statement: 'the Royal line of Wessex ruled from this day'. Many of the defeated Britons no doubt fled to what is now Dorset; the defensive earthworks of Bokerley Dyke, which still form part of the boundary between Hampshire and Dorset, probably date from this time.

Saxon domination became complete over the next century and the Fordingbridge area became part of the Kingdom of Wessex—until its kings came to rule a unified England. The most prominent monument from this time is Breamore church, which still exhibits many Saxon features, and is believed to have been founded soon after A.D. 980.

To the local historian, 1086, the date of the Domesday Survey, is often a more important date than 1066, the actual Norman invasion. While the origin of most villages cannot be dated, we do know that most of them were in existence before the time of the survey. Attempting to estimate population from the information in Domesday Book can produce only an approximation, but it is possible to tell roughly how many households or families there were in each place for comparative purposes. The results for our area are unexpected. The settlement which was eventually to develop into Fordingbridge was still called Forde, and was tiny, with only 12 families, the same number as Breamore. Even Bickton was bigger, with eighteen. There were 31 families in Rockbourne and a surprising 33 in Burgate. However, by far the largest population was in Damerham (which included Martin) with 80 households.

Although the name 'Fordingbridge' was not yet used for the town, it was already in use for the hundred (a larger administrative unit) in the Domesday Survey. The hundred was divided into various manors, most of which correspond to present-day villages. In some cases, the history and ownership of these manors can be traced, at least partially, from the Norman Conquest up to the present time.

From late in the 13th century until 1958, the lordship of the Manor of Fordingbridge was held by the Brune family, later the Prideaux-Brunes, of Padstow in Cornwall. There is no indication that they ever had a manor house within the town. Rather they were absentee-landlords who administered their lands through bailiffs and stewards. This left the local rectors and the lords of the Manor of Burgate with a great deal of influence over the life of the town.

Burgate was one of the largest manors in area but it never developed into a sizeable village or possessed a church. In the 16th and 17th centuries, the Bulkeley family lived at Burgate Manor and they were followed by the Coventrys, who built a new manor house in the 18th century. James Coventry was an expert amateur photographer in the 1890s and some of his pictures are, technically and artistically, among the best reproduced in this book. Burgate House is now the national headquarters of The Game Conservancy.

Breamore's original manor house, which was extended in c.1284, was owned by the Earls of Devon. They visited their manor only occasionally and the house was largely abandoned by the 15th century. An Augustinian priory had been founded near the River Avon in c.1130 and within 200 years it had accumulated gifts of over half of the land in the village. The prior was consequently a person of considerable influence in the district. After the Dissolution of the Monasteries, in 1536, Breamore was purchased by William Dodington, who built Breamore House in 1580. Following a bitter legal dispute with the Bulkeleys, William committed suicide by jumping from a church tower in London. Later, at Breamore House, his daughter-in-law was murdered by her own son, who was hanged for the offence. The family fortunes never recovered and their properties came through marriage to the Brookes, later Earls of Warwick. In 1748, the house and the estates were bought by the Hulse family, who still hold the Lordship of the Manor of Breamore today. The house is open to the public during the summer months, along with an interesting Countryside Museum and Carriage Museum.

Rockbourne is a large village, mostly strung out along a single street, with considerable evidence of a planned layout dating from the 12th or 13th century. Unfortunately few documents older than the 17th century survive, but parts of the medieval manor house are still in existence. Nearby West Park originated as a medieval deer park but in 1628 was used for pasturing race-horses belonging to Charles I. In 1762 it was purchased by General Sir Eyre Coote, a contemporary of Clive of India. A monument to him still stands on a hill within the park, overlooking the Roman villa.

The Manor of Damerham (including Martin) was owned by Glastonbury Abbey—indeed, it was one of the largest and most profitable manors held by the abbey. Since its dissolution in 1539 the abbey's records have been preserved at Longleat House. Cataloguing a few years ago showed that Damerham is one of the best documented villages in the country, with remarkable series of court rolls and account rolls for the 13th to 16th centuries still in existence. As yet, little detailed research has been carried out on these records.

Other manors in the hundred of Fordingbridge which were mentioned in Domesday and which fall within our area included the Charfords, Hale, Outwick, Midgham and North Gorley. Hale was almost certainly included in one of the three Domesday entries for 'Cerdeford' (Charford). Outwick today is an outlying hamlet within Breamore parish, whilst North and South Midgham villages have been deserted since the 15th century. North Gorley, set around its village green, grazed by forest ponies and donkeys, is perhaps best known through its picturesque *Royal Oak Inn*.

By the 13th century, Fordingbridge had achieved the status of a small market town, with its hinterland extending from Breamore in the north to Gorley in the south and from Damerham in the west to Godshill in the east. Fifteen or more villages and hamlets came to look upon Fordingbridge as the local commercial and administrative centre, with its market and Hundred Court. For many of the Forest-edge hamlets, it was also the ecclesiastical centre; indeed some are still part of Fordingbridge parish today, while the others left it only in 1855. At that date, a new parish of Hyde was formed to include also Blissford, Frogham, Hungerford and North Gorley.

In Tudor times almost all of the trades and industries expected in any small rural town were to be found here, particularly those associated with leather working. Butchers, skinners, tanners, leather dressers and shoemakers are all recorded, as also are dyers, shirtmakers, brewers, bakers and mercers (general merchants in cloth, household goods and exotic foodstuffs).

Tudor Fordingbridge consisted largely of half-timbered cruck houses of late medieval date, although there were a few box-frame dwellings which belonged to the better-off inhabitants—which included the vicar. This latter type of construction became the norm as the medieval housing stock was replaced or modernised towards the end of the 16th century. Unfortunately, serious fires in the town in 1662, 1672 and 1702 ensured that none of these dwellings lasted into modern times. Only St Mary's church and the Great Bridge remain from the medieval period. The oldest house now surviving in the town is the brick-built Court House for the Manor of Burgate, of about 1600, situated near the post office and facing down Salisbury Street. Many of the buildings to be seen today date from soon after the 1702 fire. There are, however, a number of examples of half-timbering from the 17th century remaining, but these are mostly hidden away in parts of houses and shops which were partially saved from destruction.

The dramatic events of the Civil War seem almost to have passed the area by; no doubt there were troop movements but no skirmishes or battles that we know of. The Dodingtons of Breamore are known to have been Parliamentarians, as were some other local families.

Fordingbridge's market decreased in significance as permanent shops replaced market stalls in the 16th and 17th centuries. During this time the town began to expand northwards into the area which is now Salisbury Street and new buildings were added around Church Square. The town continued to support a wide variety of traders and manufacturers; by the end of the 18th century the dominant industries were the manufacture of ticking (a closely-woven fabric used for the outer casing of feather-filled pillows and mattresses) and calico printing. Nearly 500 looms were employed in producing ticking and sail-cloth at this time.

Nationally the 19th century was, of course, a time of major innovations in methods of transport resulting in increasing mobility for the general public. This trend was reflected locally in a number of ways. There was a gradual improvement in the condition of the roads; that from Southampton to Shaftesbury, passing through Godshill, Fordingbridge and Damerham became a turnpike before 1833. By this time there was a regular stage-coach service on this route, as there was on the north-south road from Salisbury to Poole. The *Greyhound Inn* in Salisbury Street and the *Crown Inn* in the Market Square were important as coaching inns. Of greater significance to most local inhabitants were the carriers' carts which provided a cheap 'bus service' between local towns and villages, particularly to the markets at Salisbury and Ringwood.

As we move into the second half of the 19th century, the local historian begins to benefit from visual evidence in the form of early photographs. It is indeed fortunate that the advent of photography came early enough to document a centuries-old way of life before it finally disappeared. In the body of this book, we have used these photographs to try to draw together the threads of life in Fordingbridge and its rural hinterland during the latter years of the 19th century—and to record some of the changes which took place as the 20th century advanced.

Many of the photographs included here were taken by the various professional photographers who lived and worked in Fordingbridge over the years. The earliest on record seems to have been William Hockey, who was active in 1875. We have not been able to include any examples of his photographs—it is not even clear whether any actually survive. By 1892 Frederick Eyras Angell had established his 'School of Photography' in Provost Street, and plates 96 and 109 are his.

In the years before the First World War, when studio photography was becoming accessible to more people, there were for the first time two photographers competing in Fordingbridge. Witcomb and Son had their studio at West End, while Albert Thomson was based at nearby Nyanza Terrace.

During the First World War and throughout the 1920s, Herbert Cheeseman had a studio in Salisbury Street. Considerably more prolific at this time, however, were Edwards and Smith of the Market Place. They took many hundreds of views of the town and surrounding villages and sold them in the form of picture postcards, which were a popular form of communication at the time. Many of Edwards and Smith's postcards are reproduced in this volume. Some of their original glass negatives survive, but most were destroyed after the firm finished trading. Many were even used as garden edging!

In addition to the obvious views of streets and villages, photographers tended to record groups such as school classes, youth groups and sports teams, as well as special events. Fortunately, they also produced photographic post-cards of people at their everyday tasks, which give us an even clearer view of life at the time.

Our earliest photograph of a school is from the 1890s, but there had been some formal education in earlier centuries. In 1687, a schoolmaster by the name of Bryan Flexney was recorded as living in Fore Street (now High Street), but we have no information about where he taught—perhaps it was in the church. Certainly, there were unofficial schoolmasters teaching in Breamore church during the 17th century.

Neither Rockbourne, Whitsbury or Breamore had a school in 1725. At the same date, Fordingbridge was said to have 'no endowed school', which may perhaps imply that there were small private establishments. The town had at least one school before the end of the 18th century and others are known during the first few decades of the 19th; most of the larger villages in the area had schoolrooms by the middle of the 19th century.

By 1840 there was a British School (non-conformist) on the site of the Victoria Rooms and this moved to Roundhill 10 years later. The National School (Church of England) had been established in Shaftesbury Street in 1835. In due course this school became the site of the town's classes for boys, girls and infants, continuing in use until the three existing schools were established to the north of the town between 1957 and 1970. The old school building is now used as the Avonway Community Centre.

Numerous small private schools have existed from time to time, both in and near the town; perhaps the most notable being the still flourishing Sandle Manor Preparatory School.

A rich ecclesiastical heritage has sustained the life of the area for centuries and churches of several denominations continue to serve their congregations. The area's medieval churches are a source of architectural and historical interest for locals and visitors alike, exhibiting examples of workmanship from every age—from the late 10th-century features of Breamore's Saxon minster to the relatively new structures at Hyde and Sandleheath. The parish of Fordingbridge is large enough still to warrant its own full-time incumbent, but some other parishes have fallen victim to declining congregations and must share vicars.

Fordingbridge has its own Roman Catholic church; while Martin, for a period of 20 years at the start of this century, was home to a community of Trappist monks. In addition to various non-conformist 'chapels' in the villages, there is a United Reformed church and a Methodist church in Fordingbridge—but the former Methodist chapel at Breamore, after a period as a dental surgery, is now a private residence.

The Quakers, properly known as the Society of Friends, were first mentioned in 1669 when their local community was still very small. By 1694 they were sufficiently well established to obtain a house and land in Back Street (now Roundhill) from one of their number, William Lumber, a local cheesemonger. In the fire of 1702 the Society lost much of its property, so a new meeting house was built in 1705. This remained in use until 1835 when the present building, now used as an auction sale-room, was erected. By the end of the 19th century membership was declining; services had largely ceased by 1905. Some 19th-century Quaker gravestones still survive alongside the sale-room.

Photographers are always busy on 'special days', so that there are ample records of weddings, coronation celebrations, carnivals and the like. Fordingbridge's carnival is still an important date in the town's calendar; but the elaborate regattas of the late 19th and early 20th centuries must have been even more spectacular events, judging by the photographs which have been preserved. Water sports had long been a favourite pastime on the Avon at Fordingbridge, with sailing events recorded by 1850 and rowing by 1870. The popularity of the regatta was such that people travelled from far afield; for a while, it was not unreasonable to mention Fordingbridge Regatta in the same breath as Henley!

Sports also thrived on the land, with clubs developing both in the town and in the villages during the Victorian period. At Rockbourne and Breamore, cricket was being played as early as the 1830s. Not long after this, the game was established in Fordingbridge, where matches were played on the field which later became the Recreation Ground.

Organised football came a little later with the formation of the Fordingbridge Football Club in 1868, one of the earliest clubs in Hampshire. The name Fordingbridge 'Turks' has an interesting origin; perhaps hoping to achieve similar feats, the club chose it in celebration of Turkish forces which overcame a vastly superior Russian force at the Battle of Plevna. Most villages had football teams before the end of the last century and some still survive. In others, such as Breamore, which had very successful sides in the first half of the century, it is no longer played.

Fordingbridge has had few direct links with the military, but photographs survive of the local Territorials and Home Guard platoons. Quasi-military youth groups like the A.T.C. were also photographed, as were local Boy Scout and Girl Guide troops.

Fordingbridge never developed major manufacturing industries, but, at Stuckton, an iron foundry was opened by the Sheppard family towards the end of the 1780s. Some of the first steam traction engines are said to have been made there early in the 19th century. (Later models of these impressive machines were always attractive to photographers!) Later the business was taken over by Joseph Armfield & Co. of Ringwood, who operated as millwrights, flour mill engineers, iron and brass founders and agricultural engineers.

In the second half of the 19th century, a number of Quaker families became very influential in the district. These included the Thomsons and Neaves, who came to prominence through their manufacturing and milling interests. Samuel Thompson & Co., canvas makers, spinners and merchants, had factories at East Mill and at West End. Josiah Neave & Co. manufactured 'farinaceous food' at their factory near Fordingbridge railway station (see plate 124).

The Salisbury and Dorset Junction Railway had reached the valley in 1865. As a result, patterns of trade and communications for most of the area were altered irreversibly. Breamore station was placed conveniently near the village, but Fordingbridge would certainly have been better served by a station nearer to the town than the site chosen, over half a mile west of the Market Square. This resulted in the development of the 'suburb' of Ashford with a number of new industries and storage depots, including Neave's factory, springing up around the station. The inevitable *Railway Hotel* was renamed the *Load of Hay* after the closure of the line in 1963.

The gas works in Back Street (now known as West Street) was built in 1866 and many of the better-off inhabitants soon had access to this new form of lighting for their homes. The town itself also benefited as, by October 1867, there were 41 public lamps installed in the streets, one of the earliest such schemes in Hampshire. In premises in the same street, for a period after the First World War, a largely female staff manufactured carpets for the Wilton Royal Carpet factory.

Shering's, still a major employer in Fordingbridge today, is a long-established family business in the town, having progressed from carpentry through related trades to major building projects.

Service industries have always been a major source of employment. There are photographs of road-makers, coal merchants, bakers, saddlers, grocers, tailors, post office staff and a variety of town and country shop-keepers—as well as the police. In the 1840s the law enforcement duties of the old manorial officials had been taken over by the new police force. The larger villages soon had their own constables, but it was inevitably Fordingbridge which became the headquarters of the local force. In 1859 a new police station was constructed at West End (where it remains in use today) with accommodation for 12 prisoners.

We have already mentioned some of the local families of landed gentry whose estates included fine country houses. For many, the Victorian and Edwardian periods were their hey-day, before all the social changes brought about largely by the First World War. Their life-style is aptly depicted by some of James Coventry's photographs. Well-to-do Victorian merchants, like Josiah Reynolds Neave, aspired to a similar life-style. Today, however, just as Coventry's manor house is used as offices, Neave's out-of-town Victorian mansion is a hospital.

Unfortunately, few photographs seem to have survived in this area of farmers and farm workers busy in the fields. However, snapshots belonging to the family of one of the authors act as a documentary record of life on a Breamore smallholding in the 1930s. The most recent picture in the book is the last which appears—a horse-drawn hay-wagon in use in 1959, photographed by Gerald Ponting, then a student.

The arrival of the tractor, together with other applications of technology to agriculture, represents just one of the major changes of the 20th century. In the years since 1945, the pace of change has increased. In particular, the rapid multiplication of the motor-car, with its numerous side-effects, has altered life-styles completely here, as in the rest of rural England.

From the 1960s onwards, the town of Fordingbridge has expanded considerably. A number of housing estates have been added to the periphery of the town, resulting in a population expansion to almost six thousand. Fordingbridge is a thriving community, with an attractive array of local shops, several churches and well-supported schools. The community holds a number of popular annual events, such as the Carnival, Spring Festival, Agricultural Show, 'Carpet of Flowers' and the late-night Shopping Festivities before Christmas.

Many local residents commute to Salisbury, Bournemouth, Southampton and elsewhere; employment in the town continues to be mainly in the service industries with a few small-scale manufacturing and craft-based businesses. Tourism is already of considerable significance to the local economy; the potential exists to increase its importance in the coming years. The by-pass, constructed in the mid-'70s, diverted much of the heavy traffic from the town centre and the narrow medieval bridge. More recently a Hampshire County Council initiative has further enhanced the urban environment of the town centre with trees, new paving and traffic-calming measures. Other developments are planned which will help to revitalise the centre of the town.

The picturesque villages around Fordingbridge have perhaps changed even more since the end of the Second World War—not in their appearance so much as in their character. In 1945, the great majority of a village's population was employed, directly or indirectly, in agriculture. Most of the inhabitants were tenants of the local estate and members of families which had lived in the same village (sometimes in the same house) for generations. With nationwide changes in farming practice, reduction of public transport and the financial pressures on large estates, this pattern broke up throughout the '50s, '60s and '70s. Large estates were split up, former farm workers moved to jobs in towns and previously tenanted cottages came onto the open market. At the same time, there was a movement of former city-dwellers into the countryside—for retirement, for weekend and holiday homes and for commuting. Labourers' cottages, sometimes semi-derelict and rarely with 20th-century conveniences, were upgraded into highly desirable residences. Refurbishment of the village housing stock (often centuries old) continues today, but there is still a need for the development of craft workshops and small rural-based industries which would provide local employment.

The village services are less essential for the more mobile new villagers—village shops, schools and even the churches are consequently engaged in a sometimes losing battle for survival. Nevertheless, a renewed community spirit has emerged in many of the villages as the talents and resources of the new families have blended with the local knowledge and experience of the old.

Whether the reader is a visitor to the area, a recently-arrived resident or a member of a family which can trace its local roots back many generations, we trust that the following collection of photographs will prove a fascinating insight into our recent past.

Fordingbridge Street Scenes

1.   Church Square, on the north side of the churchyard, was traditionally the site of Fordingbridge's annual September Fair. The roadway, curving through the right of the picture, seems to be defined only by a shallow damp gulley and a slight camber. The houses have seen few major alterations since this 1890s photograph but the appearance of the square has been transformed by modern landscaping.

2.   The Quadrant Almshouses were erected in 1909 on the site of the old calico printing works and given to the parish in 1919 by Reginald Hannen. On the opposite side of the road is Brook Terrace. At the narrow entrance into Church Square is the 17th-century cottage known as Church View. When it was demolished, house remains dating back to the 13th century were discovered.

3. The woman in the doorway of a rather dilapidated Brook Terrace, in Church Street, is thought to have been Mrs. Maidment. Wide-brimmed hats of this type became popular from about 1910.

4. The two streams of Ashford Water and Sweatford Water meet at this point and flow under Knowles' Bridge. They join the Avon near Town Mill. The bridge was named after Thomas Knowles, a local mercer, who died in 1641. His premises were on the site of the house to the left of this 1920s picture. Church Street is in the foreground and Provost Street beyond the bridge.

5. The Town Mill ground corn from the surrounding fields for many centuries. However, as with most mills, the surviving buildings are largely of 19th-century date. Those seen here were extended in 1867 when the Neave family took possession. In the Domesday Survey of 1086 two mills are recorded; both were probably here, under one roof.

6. The north-western side of Provost Street, on the left in this photograph, had been owned since the 15th century by the Provost and Scholars of King's College, Cambridge, hence the street name. Almost nothing remains of the buildings seen on this side of the Victorian street, but the opposite side has had fewer changes, the furthest building being the site of the *King's Arms*.

7. One of the latest heavy snow storms of the century blanketed much of southern England on 25 April 1908. Because it occurred so far into the spring it was much photographed. This postcard of Provost Street shows the extent to which it affected—and fascinated—the townspeople.

GREAT SNOW STORM APRIL 25TH 1908

PROVOST ST. FORDINGBRIDGE.

8. The Market Place had lost its regular markets by the early 19th century; the market-house, which stood where the lamp-post now stands, was pulled down in 1829. The shop with its blinds open in this 1920s photo was a clothiers belonging to Charles Eldridge. On the left were Horton's and then Fry's, both butchers, in an attractive late 17th-century building.

9. This 1890s view of the Market Place from Shaftesbury Street is instantly recognisable today. Both the *Royal Arms Hotel* on the right and the Town Hall, with its clock tower, are little altered. The Town Hall was built in 1876 as the Oddfellows Hall.

10.   This fine 1910 view of the High Street shows many details of the shops and houses in this part of the town. The boy with the brush is outside Alexander Brothers' Ironmongers Stores, a long established family business, which seems to be in competition with Coundley's Cycle Works opposite for business from the fledgling motor trade.

11. The Wilts and Dorset Bank replaced a row of cottages at the junction of Bridge Street and Salisbury Street in 1876. It survives today as Lloyds Bank, with few external alterations. The 'square' here held the town's markets until about 1680. The wheel on the extreme left is a shop sign for Coundley and Son's Cycle Works.

12. The river once figured much more prominently in the life of the town. One aspect of this was the row of tea gardens along the west bank, above the Great Bridge. The *Albany Hotel*, the *Greyhound Hotel* and the *Riverside Hotel* all participated, but this pleasant and relaxing way of life did not survive the Second World War.

13. The left side of the street at Horseport is dominated by the Victoria Rooms, built in 1874 on the site of the old British School. The shop opposite was run in the 1890s by a draper with the splendid name of Mr. Fairweather Fairlie. The sign above the awning suggests that his shop was called 'The Bonanza' but, strangely for a draper, he was also advertising 'Lipton's Tea'!

14. The eastern approach to the Great Bridge at Fordingbridge has been known as Horseport since at least the 14th century. Bridge House on the left was the local doctors' surgery until 1993. It stands on the site of a 16th-century mansion known as Blackhall, which later became a tavern—known successively as the *Little George* and the *Dolphin*.

15.   This 1890s view of Salisbury Street, taken from what was then known as Coventry's Corner, shows a little girl standing outside Prospect Row. These cottages were constructed from the stables of the adjoining Old Manor House. Most of the row was demolished in the 1930s for road widening.

16.   The Old Manor House still survives at the top end of Salisbury Street, although the lime trees have long gone. It was built in about 1600 as the Court House for the Manor of Burgate. The cottages on the left are now the site of the town's post office. The house on the right was the *Star Inn* in 1840.

17. The main entrance to Burgate House was this trackway from Salisbury Street, which is visible in the distance. The young girl is standing in front of the South Lodge of the house. The gas lamp by the Park Gates was one of many in the town illuminated from the gas works in Back Street (West Street), which opened in 1867.

Forest-edge Villages

18. With its one-in-three gradient, Blissford Hill has always been a considerable challenge for vehicles of all types. Until the 1930s it was regularly used for both car and motor-bike trials, and more recently pram-races have been a source of local entertainment. The cottages have been replaced now, but the hill retains its character, even with a tarmac coating.

19. In 1905, this part of Hyde was still relatively new. Although most of these houses remain, on the western edge of the Common, the scene is impossible to photograph today, being entirely obscured by trees. The furthest house on the right is now the village club.

20. This house at the top of Penton's Hill on the edge of Hyde Common is today known as 'Hanningtons'. Many of these old foresters' cottages have now been converted into more comfortable modern houses. However, the traditional construction of cob and thatch is clearly seen, at the right of the picture. The house beyond no longer exists, although the shed adjoining it has been replaced by a more modern dwelling.

21. Woodgreen Village Hall has achieved considerable fame due to the murals of village life which cover its internal walls. That depicted here shows the Flower Show. Others show fruit-picking, Morris dancers, poachers, milking a cow, the Methodist Sunday School and other village scenes. The hall was built in 1931 and the murals painted in 1932-3 by R. W. Baker and E. R. Payne, two newly qualified R.C.A. students. Both became eminent men in the art world in later life; they returned to Woodgreen for a memorable harvest supper in the hall in 1979. The murals, using villagers of the time as models, were completed in 18 months with the aid of grants from the Carnegie Trust and the Development Commission. They were conserved recently during the modernisation of the hall.

22. Ernest Harrod, Steward of Sandy Balls, by the door of the Common Room at the Riverside Camp in Sandy Balls Wood, *c.*1930. In 1919, the Sandy Balls woodland, part of Breamore Estate since the 16th century, had been purchased by the Westlake family, who still own it. Today it is a major holiday centre. See also plate 156.

23.   Members of the Order of Woodcraft Chivalry at the Great Feast held during their Folkmoot in Sandy Balls Wood, Godshill, in August 1926. The large baskets in the centre contain fruit which is about to be distributed among the members.

24.   Castle Hill near Woodgreen takes its name from the nearby small Iron-Age fortification which is surmounted by a 12th-century motte and bailey earthwork. It has long been a favourite site for Sunday afternoon walks and visitors still come both by car and on foot to admire the fine views across the Avon Valley.

Valley Villages

25.   Yew Tree Farm, like many other former farmhouses in Breamore, is now a private residence. Although documented no earlier than 1602, when it was tenanted by Valentine Edsall, the site has been occupied since medieval times. The pond in the foreground, like many others, has long since silted up.

26.   Well Cottage at Breamore was built in about 1750. It replaced a cottage built in the late 16th century on the edge of the new park surrounding William Dodington's new manor house (Breamore House). At that time this was the road to the church from the upper part of the village. The view today has changed little since the 1890s. Two young girls appear in many of James Coventry's photos (see plate 158) and were presumably members of his family. They were always placed to add artistry and interest to the picture.

27.   The Lodge House on Breamore Marsh was built in 1890; the total cost of £220 included £70 for stone and £35 for bricks. The diamond-patterned windows are characteristic of Breamore Estate cottages of the time. The road past the lodge was also relatively new, having replaced a track (just visible in the bottom right-hand corner) in order to avoid a wet area further up the hill.

28.   Breamore's ancient stocks, set on the open space of Little Marsh for centuries, were enclosed into the garden of the new village school in 1872. No doubt they served as a timely reminder of the fate awaiting unruly schoolchildren! Today they have a new site a little way along the road, opposite the *Bat and Ball*, where they can be more easily seen. The significance of the writing on the wall of the pub outhouse remains a mystery.

29.   Now a quiet little hamlet about half a mile from Breamore, Outwick once bristled with activity. Over eighty people lived here in the middle of the last century, but only three of the houses survive. One past resident, John Newman, achieved notoriety by being transported to Australia in the 1830s.

30.   The scene here at Burgate Cross, c.1930, is still recognisable today, despite many changes of detail. The road in the right foreground is now the busy A338, Salisbury-Bournemouth road. The wooden cross on the triangular green is a rare survivor of numerous others which once marked the outer bounds of Cranborne Chase.

31.   Until 1773, this entrance to Burgate House was part of the King's highway from Fordingbridge to Breamore, but enclosure of the park led to a new road (Salisbury Road) being built around its western edge, where it runs today. Both park and track have now gone and the setting of North Lodge, between the Burgate School and the Fordingbridge by-pass, is very different.

AVONSIDE, FORDINGBRIDGE.

32.   The road from Fordingbridge to Godshill runs past East Mill and the banks of the Avon before starting to climb out of the valley towards the New Forest. The scattered cottages and farms here made up the manor of Criddlestyle, which before the Norman Conquest had been part of the much larger Burgate estate.

33.   East Mill has been the site of a mill since Saxon times. By the 15th century it was used for fulling cloth, and later it was converted for the production of sail-cloth. During the anti-machinery riots of 1830 it was attacked by a mob. Many of the ring-leaders were either executed or transported.

East Mill
Fordingbridge.

34.   The quiet little village of Bickton has a history stretching back at least to Roman times. In 1303 there was a chapel here, but there are no later records of it; in more recent times villagers have had to attend church at Fordingbridge. There has been a mill at Bickton for many centuries but the present building dates from the 19th century. When this photograph was taken, from downstream on an early spring afternoon near the turn of the century, it was still being used as a corn mill by Neave & Co. (see plates 124-5).

Downland Villages

35. This strange little cottage with a verandah, photographed in 1905, stood alone by the road from Fordingbridge to Whitsbury until it was demolished about twenty years ago. Otherwise there have been few changes to this country lane apart from the inevitable coat of tarmac.

36. The tranquility of this scene in Whitsbury village street is hard to appreciate today, even in this relatively quiet village. Although the inevitable changes to trees and hedgerows over more than eighty years make this scene almost unrecognisable today, all of the buildings seen here survive. The Primitive Methodist chapel on the left was erected in 1901.

Whitsbury.
47.

37. This view of the village of Rockbourne village clearly shows its setting within a narrow valley cut into the chalk downlands. Most of the houses are on the valley floor, flanking a single street, but the church is cut into the hillside overlooking them. Just to the right of the church are several surviving buildings from the medieval manorhouse.

38. The fitful chalk stream still flows along Rockbourne street, at least in winter, although its edges are no longer trampled and muddied by cattle. The village layout is largely medieval in origin, although only a few of the picturesque cottages there today pre-date the 17th century.

39. It is now summer, and the level of the Rockbourne stream has dropped considerably. Usually at this time of the year the bed is completely empty until autumn rains replenish it. The muddy roads of winter have been replaced by summer dust.

40. This wonderfully evocative photograph, taken around the turn of the century by James Coventry, shows South End, Damerham. The scene is now identified only with difficulty, as the furthest house has gone and bushes and trees have considerably changed the appearance of the area. The manor of Damerham Parva, to which South End belonged, was owned by the Shaftesbury family of Wimborne St Giles between 1685 and 1856.

41. The two little girls posing here would find it difficult to recognise this group of cottages at Damerham Mill End today. The house on the left has gone and the one beyond the cart has been radically altered. The Mill House just visible on the right is one of two mill sites known in the village, although there are said to have been as many as four in medieval times.

42.   Damerham, the largest of the local villages, has a long and interesting history. The little bridge over the Allen Water gave its name to this street. Beyond the bridge, at East End, the building with the prominent chimneys is the *Compasses Inn*, still popular today. When this picture was taken, the house on the extreme right was used as the post office.

43.   This house, Woodview at East End, Damerham, has changed little over the years. Even the porch is still there, although it has since acquired a gable roof. The advertisement on the right is for the repair of all models of 'Singer Sewing Machines'.

44.   The picturesque village of Martin is largely set along a single street, with the turning to the left leading to Martin Down, now a National Nature Reserve. In 1266, King Henry III granted the Abbot of Glastonbury, as lord of the Manor of Martin, the right to hold a weekly market at this cross on Wednesdays and an annual fair on 29 June.

45.   College House, in the background, is thought to have been the Martin village poor house in the 19th century; there was no connection with a university, as is usual with such names. According to the Poor Law Records it was re-thatched in 1800 at a cost of £5 15s. 9d. The footpath on the right ran the whole length of the village, but has since grassed over.

Schools and Churches

46. Harbridge School lies on the edge of the green belonging to the hamlet of Turmer, hidden away within Somerley Park. Even for the purposes of this photo, taken in about 1895, the boys are carefully segregated from the girls.

47. Class II of the Fordingbridge Girls School, c.1908. The National School was opened in 1835 and extended as the elementary school in 1880. By 1897 it had been further enlarged to accommodate 140 boys, 147 girls and 189 infants.

48. The staff and pupils of Martin School assemble in the playground to have their photograph taken in about 1910. The school was closed some years ago and the building is now a private house. Present-day Martin children attend the Western Downland School which has two sites, at Damerham and Rockbourne.

49. Members of the Godshill Sunday School about to put all thoughts of the impending war in Europe out of their minds with a bone-jarring day trip to Bournemouth in a solid tyred lorry, during the summer of 1914. The Godshill Mission church had only been built in the previous year, although a mission room had existed previously.

50. The pupils of Godshill School in 1924. Cecil Cutler, on the extreme right of the back row, later became a member of the Woodgreen Morris Dancers (see plate 101).

51.   A class of happy looking children at Fordingbridge School in 1930. Many of these faces are still familiar around the area today. The old school building is now occupied by the Avonway Community Centre.

52.   The junior class of Breamore School in 1947. We have been able to name all those shown, as one of the authors is in this group! Back row, left to right: Sylvia Clements, Gordon Clampit, Keith Harrison, Eliza Turner, Jean Crowson, Michael Mayhew, Wendy Isaacs; middle row: Shirley Isaacs, Rodney Biffen, Henry Cooper, Marion Laws, Michael Edden, Betty Harrington, Hugh Mitchell, Michael Shugar, Joyce Conduct; front row: Wendy Light, Paul Biffen, Gerald Ponting, Janet Light, Geoffrey Marks, Doreen Cross, Ray Edden.

53. This view of Fordingbridge church from the south east clearly shows the old mansard-shaped nave roof before its reconstruction during the major restoration of the church in 1901-3. The chancel was also restored by King's College, Cambridge in 1903 and a choir vestry added on the south side.

54. This picture of St Mary's, Fordingbridge, from the south west, taken in about 1925, is unusual in that it shows the old west gate into the churchyard, which once gave the occupiers of the vicarage, seen on the extreme left, easy access to the church via the west door.

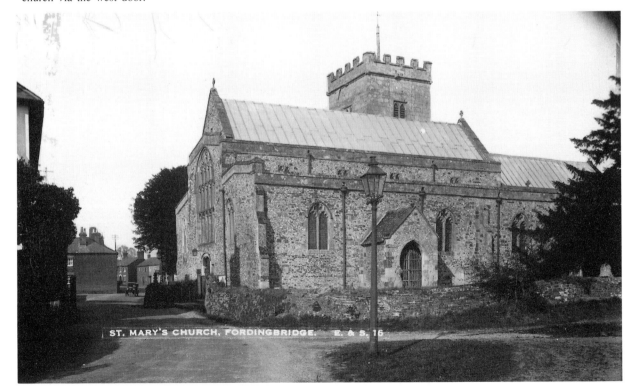

ST. MARY'S CHURCH, FORDINGBRIDGE.   E. & S. 16

Congregational Chapel, Fordingbridge.

55.   The Congregational chapel in Salisbury Street (now the United Reformed church) was built in 1832. However, a chapel had been established soon after 1662 on this half an acre of ground, previously owned by the Hospital of St Cross at Winchester. The iron railings, like so many others, were removed during the Second World War. The old manse can be seen at the back.

56.   This splendid view of Breamore church was taken before the major restoration of 1897 which led to the discovery of the church's Saxon origins. The chancel had already been repaired in 1874. The wooden grave markers on the left have now gone, but one decayed example still survives to the north of the church.

57. To the west of Rockbourne church lies a group of buildings which once formed part of the medieval manor-house complex (see plate 37). The old chapel shown here dates from the 13th century, but has for centuries been used as a barn. The big barn just visible on the left is 145ft. long and dates from the 15th century.

58. The Church of the Holy Ascension at Hyde was built of red brick in 1855 when a new parish was carved out of the (very large) old parish of Fordingbridge. The east window was added in 1875 by Rev. Warren in memory of his parents. There were originally seats for 230 people, the population of the parish in 1901 being 754.

59. In 1901, Bustard Farmhouse was occupied by Trappist monks of Our Lady of Paradise, an order of Cistercian monks. They farmed not only Bustard Farm, but nearby King's Farm as well. Their stay was a short one, however, as in 1920 they left, and the burials in their graveyard were re-interred elsewhere.

60. The Cistercian monks at Bustard Farm in Martin built their own Roman Catholic church soon after their arrival in 1901. After their departure in 1920, the church was taken down, sold, and re-erected as the garrison church at Bulford army camp in Wiltshire.

Special Days

61.   This group of guests at Gillian Quertier's wedding was photographed in the gardens of Oaklands, near Parsonage Farm, in August 1901. The Quertiers were a prominent local family of the time. Adolf Quertier & Co. were oatmeal merchants at Railway Buildings, whilst A. & J. Quertier grew fruit at the adjoining Ashford Vineries.

62.   This little group of local children, including William Shering (fourth from left), are pictured behind the Town Hall, dressed as nursery rhyme characters. The event is uncertain, but is possibly the Edward VII coronation celebrations in 1902. Characters, from left to right: Little Jack Horner, Jack and Jill, Old Mother Hubbard, Little Bo Peep, Miss Muffet, Ride-a-cock-horse, Little Boy Blue, Red Riding Hood, Dick Whittington and Mary, Mary, Quite Contrary.

63.   When 'Mr. W. H. McArdle's monoplane' landed in a field near Fordingbridge on 19 July 1910, it was indeed a special day! The beginnings of powered flight were a source of great fascination; for many locals this would have been their first sight of an aeroplane, less than seven years after the Wright brothers first flew successfully. Presumably it managed to take off again!

64.   In celebration of the 1911 coronation, an arch of greenery dominates Shaftesbury Street. In the background it is clear that the Town Hall has the letters 'G.R.' emblazoned across its balcony. On the right, Miss Elfrida Tiller's confectionery shop bears the words 'May the Eternal Power bless the Temporal Power of George Our King'.

65.   Every community went to great lengths to celebrate the coronations of the early 20th century and Fordingbridge was certainly no exception. Decorations and flags were festooned across almost every house and shop, while elaborate archways were built, as here in Church Square in 1911. Portraits of King George V and Queen Mary are incorporated in the tops of the double arch.

66. A grey and damp day dawns for the Coronation festivities on 22 June 1911 but flags, floral wreaths and shrubs decorate the High Street. On the right, Foster's greengrocer's and confectioner's shop (now the fishmonger's) and Emily Street's stationer's (now Harrison's) both played their part.

67. The procession which accompanied the 1911 coronation celebrations was enlivened by the music of the Fordingbridge Coronation Clowns' Band. The picture here was taken at the back of the pavilion in the Recreation Ground—where nearly all such processions began or ended.

68. For the peace celebrations in 1919, the Breamore House fire brigade turned out in full uniform, with the horse-drawn engine bedecked with flags and garlands. The driver is Harry Read. Back row, left to right; Ted Downer?, -?-, ? Warner?, Bill Dyer, -?-; front row: -?-, Joe Nicklen, Fred Trim, Walter Trim.

69.   The end of hostilities in 1918 was marked in almost every village and town by festivities and parades. At Breamore, the fête was held in the park; here the line of rather self-conscious youngsters is awaiting the judging of the fancy dress.

70.   At Fordingbridge the celebrations for George V's Silver Jubilee in 1935 included a carnival procession. Here it is being led through an apparently deserted Shaftesbury Street by the local police sergeant.

71. Jack Nanson and Nora Witt were married at Breamore church in 1939 and are seen here at Home Farm after the service. The bridesmaids are Brenda Waterman and Dorothy Northway, whilst the best man is Cecil Parker. Mrs. Bryant is watching through the doorway of Home Farm.

72. A Tramps' Ball was held in the Town Hall at Fordingbridge in about 1948. There are many well known local faces amongst the participants including, on the extreme left, Ben Mellor, the baker, and Geoff Brown, the fishmonger.

73. In the 1950s the annual village flower show was still held in Breamore Park. Here, some of the entrants for the fancy dress parade line up around Jack Gilbert's model house. This was designed so that Jack could walk around in it, smoking inside, so providing smoke rising out of the chimney!

74. As part of the Coronation celebrations in 1953, Fordingbridge Cottage Hospital at Highfield held a tea party for children who had been born there since it had opened in 1948. The little group at the bottom right includes, from left to right: Muriel Coleman, Joan Lever, Janet Lever, Rosemary Coleman and Graham Coleman.

75. During Breamore's 1953 Coronation celebrations, a bevy of village lovelies, calling themselves 'The Upper Street Belles', rode in style in one of the village wagons. They later took part in a tug-of-war. Stan Ponting is leading his horse 'Whitefoot', ridden by Geoffrey Lloyd; Tony Pearce perches at the rear. In the wagon are, left to right: Mary Hopper, Joan Trim, Rose Mussell, Mrs. Marlowe, Florrie Hall, Mrs. Barron, Edie Ponting, Ivy Lawes, Betty Beck, Mrs. Neave, Eileen Beck, Margaret Skeats.

Regatta and Carnival

76. Inaugurated in 1889, Fordingbridge Regatta was held on the River Avon each August until 1928. It soon became the event of the year, with water sports of every kind. This photograph of the 1904 event shows the Fordingbridge Rowing and Swimming Club boat house, with competitors preparing for their events and spectators assembled in the grandstand.

77. Fordingbridge Regatta was a great social event during the Edwardian era, with spectators travelling from far and wide—and dressing for the occasion. Boaters and wide brimmed hats for the ladies were the fashion of the time. The event became so celebrated that special trains were run from London, to what became known as the 'Hampshire Henley'.

78. Here, in about 1905, the competitors in the Senior Sculls are approaching the finish near the Boat Club, having started upstream near the Great Bridge. The rowing boats alongside the bank are largely occupied by lady spectators in their finery.

79. There were many novel events at the annual regatta, such as 'diving for plates', 'dog races!', 'pillow fights' and 'greasy pole fights'. Here, in 1907, a see-saw is set up on a rowing boat. Presumably the object was to dislodge your opponent into the river!

80-83. One of the peculiarities of the regatta was that a humorous banner was always erected over the entrance to Shering's yard, which was also the lane to the boat house. A selection of four of these banners is shown here. The strange mention of 'getting up on alternate days', refers to a contemporary piece of rivalry between Ringwood and Fordingbridge. Ringwood people accused the people of Fordingbridge of lazing in bed on alternate days. This had arisen some years previously from the habits of Howard Withers, a local shopkeeper. He occasionally spent a whole day in the *Greyhound Hotel* meeting travelling salesmen—and would spend the next day in bed to recover!

84.   One of the entrants for the illuminated boat competition is ready. The helpers pose for their photo to be taken by Albert Thomson of Nyaza Terrace, as they wait for darkness to fall and their event to begin.

85.   The day's events continued into the evening with the procession of illuminated boats and a competition for the best illuminated riverside garden. In 1909, the first prize for the latter has been awarded to Charles Neave of Southampton House (see plate 91).

FORDINGBRIDGE CARNIVAL 1923

FORDINGBRIDGE CARNIVAL 1923

FORDINGBRIDGE CARNIVAL 1923

86-88.   The 1923 carnival seems to have been particularly well photographed. The first picture shows the crowd spilling over the bridge and past the Victoria Rooms in the wake of the procession, whilst the others are of participants in the fancy dress parade, in that part of the Recreation Ground which is now the children's play area. In the background of the picture which includes two prams, crowds are still lining the street to see the remainder of the procession.

89.   By the mid-1950s, all carnival floats were motorised rather than horse-drawn and here Jeff Witt drives slowly past St John's Farm opposite the Recreation Ground. The scene here has changed considerably now, following construction of the embankment for the Fordingbridge by-pass.

Sport and Leisure

90.   The Fordingbridge Turks Football Club had been established for about twenty years when this picture of a rather casual looking team was taken in about 1890. The days of identical kit for the whole team do not seem to have arrived yet, although a photograph dated 1881 shows a much smarter team.

91. Charles Neave, of the well known milling family, pictured in his Fordingbridge Turks football kit in 1883, when he was 23 years old. He was a member of the Turks team which won the Basingstoke Cup three times between 1879 and 1881. Charles lived in Southampton House, adjoining the Great Bridge.

92.   By the 1904-5 season the whole Turks team looks much better turned out and organised. Here they are proudly displaying their cup and medals as winners of the Salisbury Junior League. One member of this team, Frank Jefferis, was signed by Southampton Town Football Club in the following season and went on to play for Preston in the 1926 F.A. Cup final.

93.   In 1885, a rival club, the Avon Rovers, was formed. Here the team of about 1905 is pictured outside the old wooden pavilion at the Fordingbridge Recreation Ground.

94. At the turn of the century the Drapers of Fordingbridge played the Butchers at the Recreation Ground, although it is not clear whether this was an annual event. At the time the town had six butchers' and six drapers' shops, each no doubt with many young male shop assistants, so it was obviously not too difficult to select the teams.

95. In the 1920-1 season, the Breamore village football team 'swept the board' in the Salisbury and District League. They won all of their 17 matches, scoring 90 goals, with only eight scored against them throughout the whole season. A large framed copy of this picture still hangs in the village hall to commemorate this achievement. Back row, left to right: Cliff Young (secretary), Arthur Blunden, Ted Edsall, Wilfie Jones, Jeff Hall, Harry Read; middle row: Bob Biddlecombe, Stan Hall, R. Hanham, T. Crouter, Cliff Witt; front row: Len Edsall, Henry Stanford, 'Krujer' Dommett (with 29 goals to his credit), Jack Biddlecombe and George Biddlecombe.

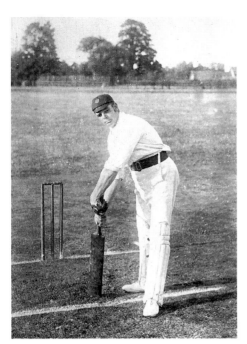

96. Charles Hood, the local coal merchant, had played football for the Turks in his youth, but his great passion was cricket. He was something of an all-rounder although, from his bowling figures, this seems to have been his stronger role. He played for both Fordingbridge and Breamore. The photograph was mounted as a 'cabinet print' (4in. by 6in.) by Fred Angell of 'The School of Photography, Fordingbridge' in 1892.

97. This splendid photo of two cricket teams was taken at Breamore in about 1895. The marquee appears to have been used as a pavilion before a permanent structure was built. The cricketers shown include Charles Hood, who is holding the ball (sitting, front row, second from right). This print was presented to Charles by Sir Edward Hulse of Breamore House.

98.   In 1922, the Fordingbridge Cricket Club was running two teams, with rather mixed results. On 28 May the first team against Hale (most of whom must appear in this picture) was: E. D. Stanford, J. Court, C. Burgess, J. G. Backus, E. Rutherford, B. Gilbert, A. Hopkins, B. Pinhorn, C. Swatridge, G. Lonnen, E. Hanham.

99.   Breamore's cricket team of about 1924, pictured outside the flint and thatch pavilion on Breamore Marsh. Walt Trim was the umpire. Back row, left to right: Harry Read, Bob Biddlecombe, George Biddlecombe, Wilf Jones; middle row: Jim Stanford, Arthur Blunden, Harry Stanford, Walt Bailey, Jeff Hall; front row: Ted Edsall, Harry(?) Blunden, Stan Hall.

100. Morris dancing has been popular in the area for many years. This postcard shows a small crowd watching a display taking place in Church Square, Fordingbridge during the 1920s. Twenty or more dancers are taking part in this dance—an occasion when several New Forest sides combined to produce a larger group.

101. The Woodgreen Morris Dancing side which reached the final stages of a national competition and thus performed at the Royal Albert Hall on Saturday, 4 January 1930. Back row, left to right: ? Chapman, A. Vincent, B. Stapley, Ernest Ponting; front row: Cecil Cutler, J. Morris, ? Stapley, A. Brewer.

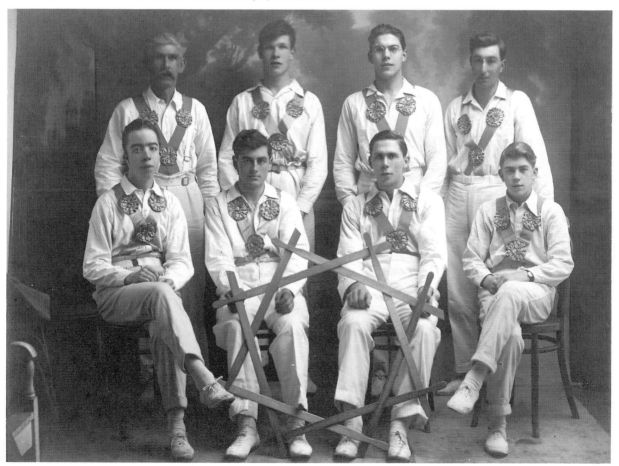

102.   The Fordingbridge church choir on their annual outing, *c*.1930. Their usual destination was Weymouth. In the centre, at the back, is George Britton, choirmaster, who was the headmaster of Fordingbridge School (in the building now used by Avonway) from 1910-43. Their transport is one of Albert Broad's 'Coo-ee Coaches'; the driver, on the left, is Les Cousins.

103.   Albert Chafen Broad ran his local motor coach business from his Salisbury Road premises during the 1920s and '30s. Here, the large staff of William King and Sons' various shops and warehouses are on their annual outing in about 1927. King's had premises in both Salisbury Street and the High Street (see plate 126). (These are just two of numerous surviving pictures of Broad's charabancs on day trips for local groups.)

104.   Pictured at the end of their first season (1928) at the Stuckton Road ground, where the Fordingbridge Bowling Club still plays today, the members are, back row, left to right: H. Shering, L. C. Mellor, H. E. Bailey, A. Coppock, A. E. Lloyd, T. Hudson, H. G. Beach (secretary), W. S. Harding (Vice-Captain), W. J. Charles (Captain), A. T. M. Hewitt, H. Hood, J. W. Shering, F. C. Pye, R. A. Munday; front row: C. Riddick, A. J. Bedford, G. P. King, A. J. Bailey, L. J. Neave, G. Parberry, D. H. Neave (President), A. T. King, C. J. Eldridge, A. E. Gilbert, H. E. Pitt, W. Taylor, H. G. Bryant; seated on the ground: W. E. Edwards, A. Whapshare.

105. Sandy Balls in the 1930s was a
haven of peace and quiet, an ideal place
for Ernest Harrod, right, to enjoy a game
of chess on a summer's day. Today, Sandy
Balls is a large and thriving holiday centre
with visitors from all over the country
and abroad enjoying its still pleasant, but
much busier, atmosphere.

106. A large crowd has gathered at a hunt meet in Provost Street shortly after the end of the Second World War. The two nurses in the background are standing in the garden of the old Nursing Home and Cottage Hospital which was closed in 1948. Opposite is the original Nicklen's garage.

107. This rowing boat belonged to the Coventry family at Burgate and features in a number of photos of the time. It was apparently used by family and guests alike for a gentle trip down the river. Here an un-named cleric is returning upstream from the shallows below the Great Bridge.

Military and Youth Groups

108.   The Fordingbridge Congregational Sunday School band of 1890. Back row, left to right: Ernest Waters, W. Holley, L. Withers, E. Young, C. Trickle, E. Coundley, W. Grove, W. Parker; middle row: George Witt, E. Hayward, G. Horsey, W. Morrell, G. Horsey; front row: Fred Coundley, C. Blackmore, G. S...ell, C. Hounsell, W. Grove, -?-, -?-, ? Hounsell, W. Wing.

109.   Fordingbridge boys dressed in the uniforms of the Volunteers of the Fourth Battalion Hampshire Regiment—though there seems a large variation in head-gear! The occasion is uncertain, but is possibly the Diamond Jubilee of Queen Victoria on 22 June 1897.

110.   A crowd of townsfolk, mostly men and boys, has gathered in the field below the Recreation Ground to watch the Second Carbineers Brigade swimming their horses across the River Avon.

111. The Seventh Battalion, Hampshire Regiment of the Territorials outside Fordingbridge Drill Hall, *c.*1910. Back row, left to right: -?-, A. E. Gilbert?, W. A. Smith, -?-, H. King, Ern King, -?-, Percy King, -?-, ? Harris?, Chas. Alexander; middle row: F. C. Pye, Sid Bailey, W. Heading, A. Clements with dog 'Jellicoe', G. Jones, W. Hicks, R. A. Luffman, T. Parker?, Geof. Britton, W. Green; front row, seated: C. J. Eldridge, W. Stevens, R. A. Munday, H. G. Beach, ? Channer?, Col. H. P. Greenwood, G. Witt, H. Neave, H. E. Kenchington, ? Norris.

112 & 113.   Both Boy Scouts and Girl Guides have from time to time featured strongly in the life of the Fordingbridge community, as in any town. This postcard of the scouts is annotated with the surnames of the troop, many of them well known in the district. The guides met in the old Church Hall. In 1926 their secretary was Mrs. Drake and their captain was Miss Hoffman of Bowerwood. There was also a guide company at Hyde.

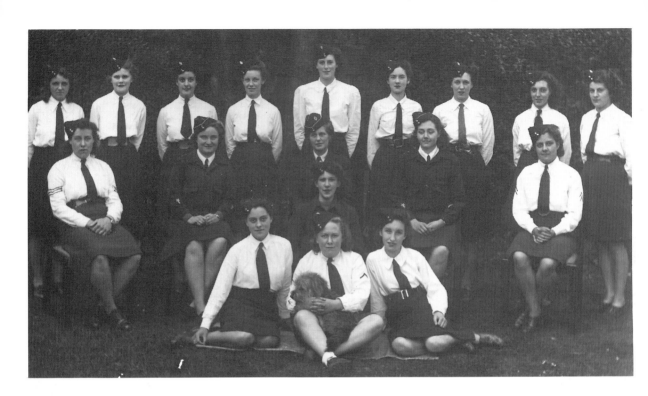

114. *(above left)* The Fordingbridge branch of the Girl's Training Corps, which met in the old primary school and which was intended for school leavers who were not yet old enough to join the regular forces. Back row, left to right: Norah Windless, Joyce Hanham, Marjory Rowlatt, Barbara Calas, Nancy Parker, Nellie Downer, Doreen Windless, Jean Lawes, Jean Damant; middle row: Lorna Knight, Daisy Harris, Mrs. Bates with Betty Bailey below, Edith Overill, Jean Rogers; front row: Edna Bessant, Joan Langdown (holding an un-named dog), Dorothy Burton.

115. *(below left)* The Breamore unit of the Local Defence Volunteers, soon to be renamed the Home Guard, in full uniform outside of the village cricket pavilion on Breamore Marsh, *c.*1940. (A later photograph shows 45 members.) From 1940 until its disbandment on 31 December 1945 the unit prepared for possible invasion by Germany and manned strategic points such as the pill-box at Breamore Mill. Back row, left to right: Wilf Bailey, Reg Sutton, ? Gunton, Bob Biddlecombe, Bill Dymott, George Young, Stan Ponting; middle row: Albert Northway, Henry Stanford, ? Montague, George Biddlecombe, Geoff Hall, George Tanner; front row: Cliff Witt, Frank Frowd, Reg Mussell, Ern Isaacs, Harold Witt.

116. *(above)* The Fordingbridge Air Training Corps Band, *c.*1945. Back row, from left to right: Percy Marlow, ? Dodds, Charlie Gouge, John Shering, Gerry Dommett, Phil Sutton, John Gould, Ron Crook; middle row: Norman Northway, Mr. Presley (bandmaster), Jim Wort; front row: -?-, Ken Harding, Billy Ings, Alan Zebedee.

At Work

117. Fred Wort with his father John's horse and cart, loaded with flint in Gorley gravel pit. The flint was brought from the chalk downlands and stockpiled ready for use in road building.

118. John Wort's road gang spreading flint on the road at the bottom of Station Hill, near the Marl Lane turning, *c*.1925; the days of tarmacadam had not yet arrived. The roller was owned by the Eddison Steam Rolling Co. Ltd. of Dorchester.

119. Bob Wort of Gorley leading his horse 'Vintner' as they move a steamroller driver's 'living van' using two horses working in tandem. Robert's father, John, is walking alongside the van. In the days of steamrollers, a driver of these vehicles needed to be an itinerant worker, moving his 'home' (and wife!) from job to job around the countryside.

120. In 1920 the steep hill between Fordingbridge and Godshill at Criddlestyle Hollow (a name now often contracted to 'Crystal Hollow') was widened by Messrs. Wort of Gorley. Here the southern bank has almost been completed; today it is covered by trees and vegetation. The motor-cycle on the left belongs to the foreman who is a little further up the hill talking to the men.

121.   The Fordingbridge water cart in Church Street, alongside Ashford Water, *c*.1925. Until the advent of tarmacadam on the town streets in the 1930s, dry roads often needed to be dampened in order to keep the dust from flying.

122.   Mr. Lawes pauses with the Armfield's of Stuckton traction engine during chalk haulage work in about 1925. (See also caption 170.)

123. Charlie Hood's coal business was established by his father Alfred in 1866 at the railway station yard. His hut, shown here, lasted for many years; the board bears an advertisement, not only for coal and coke, but also for hay and straw. Charlie's passion for cricket is shown in plates 96 and 97.

124. The staff of Neave's Food, at their factory near Fordingbridge railway station, *c.*1930. This was situated behind the public house now known as the *Load of Hay*. Here their farinaceous (cereal-based) food packing business, mainly baby foods, was established in the middle of the last century.

125.   Three of Neave and Co.'s steam lorries at Bickton, *c*.1910. These were a regular sight on the roads around Fordingbridge as they transported meal from the various mills owned by the family to the packaging factory near the railway station.

126.   Charles Nead ready to leave from King's Yard with Viney and King's delivery wagon loaded with bread, *c*.1900. Albert Bailey is behind the cart. The firm had been established before 1875 as grocers and provision merchants. By the turn of the century they had premises in Salisbury Street, Bridge Street and High Street.

127. This lady, who signs herself 'H.T.M.' on the back of the postcard, is delivering bread for John Briant of Godshill during the First World War. Her short message includes the comment 'how is this for war work?'.

128. Harold Church took over the Godshill village shop and bakery from John Briant. He is seen here on the left with his staff beside their delivery van. Aside from his bakery, Harold was also well known in the district as a breeder of poultry.

129 & 130. At least eight generations of the Shering family, stretching back through two centuries, have been engaged in the carpentry trade. The firm continues to flourish today as builders and developers, under the direction of Mr. Richard Shering. These two photos of Messrs. Shering's staff at the turn of the century show the builders and contractors above and the carpenters below. Third from the left in the group of carpenters is George Jefferies, whose apprenticeship indenture is preserved in the Shering Museum.

131.   Local workmen busy filling in the shuttering for a new weir across the River Avon at Charford in 1913. The man with the wheelbarrow is believed to be Laurie Marks, whilst Walt Trim is behind him. To the right, with the suit and boater, is the architect in charge of the project.

132.   Behind Breamore House today, close to the stables which are now used as a carriage museum, stands an ornate ivy-clad water tower. This was fed from a well. This picture shows the team of local men who deepened the well in 1906, including J. Slade, F. Edsall, ? Crouter, Bill Dyer, F. Slade, J. Frowd, Bill Harris, ? Arney, Bill Webber, J. Downer, Bill Dymott, J. West.

133.	After the First World War the famous Wilton carpet factory acquired premises in Back Street for the production of carpets. This photo shows the staff in 1923, with the forewoman in the middle of the front row. All the girls are shown, except the one who wrote the caption on the back of the print—'I'm the only one not there through being on the club'. Back row, left to right: Evelyn Andrews, Vi Davis, Jud Downer, Lil Service, Kate Kenchington, Bessie Hounsell, Miriam Wyatt, Ruby Cheater, Ethel Kenchington; front row: Daise Gosney, Glad Lockyer, Elsie Beckinham, Florie Thomas, Miss Kenchington, Phil Jefferies, Molly Parker, Win Chubb, Flora Gouge.

134.	Kit Kenchington, Glad Lockyer and Flo Zebedee of the Royal Carpet Works, with the forewoman (Miss Kenchington) at the back, at work on a carpet for the *Aquitania*. The photograph was taken on 1 May 1922 and the caption records that it was a 'cerice' [*sic*] carpet—'Plain Centre with Border'. Carpets were also made at the works for the *Lusitania* and the *Mauretania*. One carpet was so large that a hole had to be made in a gable wall, in order to remove it.

135. The laundry in Church Square was begun by Owen Eastwell early this century and later taken over by Horace Willets. By 1939 the Model Laundry was offering a 48-hour dry cleaning service and a valet service from Mr. Buckley's shop in the High Street. This interesting shot of the equipment inside the laundry was taken *c.*1925.

The ✿ ✿

Model Laundry,

CHURCH ST., FORDINGBRIDGE.

SPECIAL FEATURES—

Large 'Fitted' Drying and Airing Rooms,
—— 2 Acres Drying Grounds. ——

Pure Soft Water and Best Materials only used.
Good Work and Prompt Delivery guaranteed.

A postcard will ensure prompt attention.
Price List on application to the Proprietor.

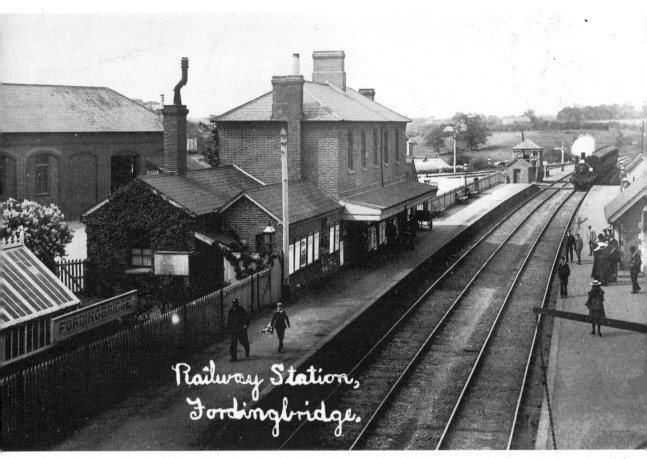

Railway Station,
Fordingbridge.

136.   A view of Fordingbridge station from the Sandleheath Road arch, *c.*1910. A steam train from Wimborne bound for Salisbury is just approaching the 'up' platform where about a dozen passengers are waiting. The boy, carrying a bouquet of flowers, walking along the down platform with a porter is Percy Fanner. The goods yard and buildings are on the left.

137.   The 11 members of the staff of Fordingbridge railway station pictured on the station forecourt, *c*.1925. In 1927 the station master was John George Lillington.

138.   The eight members of staff of Fordingbridge railway station in 1935. For most of its length the line from Wimborne to Salisbury was single track only, until it joined the Southampton to Salisbury line at Alderbury Junction. Despite its emptiness here, the station was still a busy place; the motor-car had not yet succeeded in drawing away its passengers.

139. The staff of Fordingbridge post office at the rear of their old Salisbury Street premises (now Barclays Bank) in 1930. The post-master, Mr. Pontin, is in the centre wearing a wing collar. In the 1930s, hours of opening were 8 a.m. to 7.30 p.m. daily and 9 a.m. to 10.30 a.m. on Sundays. Post-boxes were cleared at 6.15 a.m. and 2 p.m. for local delivery the same day.

140. The staff of Breamore post office, c.1925. This purpose-built post office was erected in 1913 to replace the old one in a cottage near the Woodgreen turning; it is now a private house. The four people in the middle are the Duell family: daughter Amy, Mrs. Duell, son Harry and Jimmy Duell, the village post-master.

141.   A group of five local 'bobbies' from the 1920s. Standing are P.C. Collins, the Breamore village policeman, and P.C. Johnny Newman. Seated, apparently very comfortably, are P.C. Jock Mackenzie, Sgt. John Mellor and P.C. Tom Cousins.

142.   A sale of furniture and contents at Brympton House, Sandleheath in 1955. The auctioneer is the late A. T. Morley Hewitt, the well-known local antiquarian. He was responsible for excavating the Rockbourne Roman Villa and his 1966 volume *The Story of Fordingbridge in Fact and Fancy* did much to encourage interest in the area's local history.

143. Tom Jefferis at his sewing machine in his tailor's premises in Provost Street shortly after the turn of the century. Standing at his elbow, with a tape measure around his neck, is his brother.

144.   Charles Thomas Arney's saddler's shop in Salisbury Street, seen here *c.*1910, had been opened towards the end of the last century, in part of what is now Fox & Sons office. After the First World War, the business was taken over by Alfred William Thorne who, in 1939, was advertising 'Light and heavy harness made on the premises, and repairs of every description'.

145.   Walter Andrews outside his 'Renu Boot Repairing Depot' in Provost Street (near the present-day Nicklen's garage). Rolls of leather line the front of the shop and there are adverts for 'Gripwell Boot Studs' and 'Daymar Polishes'. A sign high up on the left announces 'Sewing Machine Orders Taken Here', whilst *Army Surgeon* is showing at the Palace.

146.   Edwin Arnold standing with his son in the doorway of his shop in Salisbury Street, *c.*1910. Edwin was the brother of Annie Arnold, who ran the stationer's shop and post office in the High Street, now Forest Fruits, until 1926.

147.   From Salisbury Street, Edwin Arnold moved his business to larger premises in the High Street. His shop window display here clearly shows a string of picture postcards for sale! On the door is a poster advertising the Noel Coward play *Bitter Sweet*, first produced in 1929, which was then on show at the Southampton Empire (now the Mayflower).

148. Joseph Frisby's boot warehouse in Fordingbridge High Street, near Bank Corner, was opened before the First World War. By 1926, it had moved further up the street to premises near the present-day Leo's supermarket. 'Cosy Slippers', 'Leather Boots', 'Dress and Evening Shoes', 'Chrome Calf Boots', 'Football Boots' and 'Leggings and Gaiters' are all advertised, at prices ranging from 2s. 11d. to 12s. 6d.

149. Standing outside Samuel Witt's grocery store in Station Road, *c.*1930, are, from left to right: Vi. Jerrard, Vi. Treagus, Norah Witt and Mrs. Witt. In 1964 it was taken over by a Mr. Rhymer. Later owners have renamed it Ashford Stores.

150.   The village shop, now Breamore Stores, was built *c*.1895 by George Kilford, grocer and baker. The children are standing next to the delivery cart belonging to Kilford's successor, Thomas Vince. The hedge on the right surrounds the blacksmith's detached garden; his house and smithy are just out of the picture. The thatched cow-shed has long-since disappeared.

151.   By the 1950s ownership of the Breamore shop had passed to Bert Candy and his smart new van is standing by the bus-stop. Bread was baked at the rear of the shop and, with groceries and other household goods, was delivered to homes in Breamore, Whitsbury, Burgate and Woodgreen. Two hand-operated petrol pumps stand outside the smithy, just beyond the car parked under the 'spreading chestnut tree'.

152. Pressey's Corner, Alderholt, is named from Bert Pressey who once ran the village shop. Here, probably just before the turn of the century, an earlier proprietor, James William Palmer, poses outside the shop with his son George (the middle of the boys) who continued the trade. George Palmer died in 1991 at the age of ninety-eight. The shop is now the Moonacre Restaurant.

153. Packbridge Cottage in the foreground of this picture was Fred Hacker's first village shop, *c*.1933, before his move to Martin Cross. In the doorway of the shop is Fred's wife, Winnie. In the background, the Damerham road into Martin is already flanked by council houses.

Landowners and Merchants, their Homes and Families

154. Josiah Reynolds Neave, son of Josiah Neave of Bickton Mill, did much to expand the family milling business in Fordingbridge, but died at only 44 years of age on 2 March 1879. The original of this photograph is a 'carte de visite', a style which became extremely popular in the 1860s. The actual print, on very thin paper, measures 2½in. by 3in. and is mounted on a slightly larger stiff card. The simplicity of the design on the back, giving the photographer's details, suggests an 1860s date.

155. Highfield House at Bowerwood, between Fordingbridge and Alderholt, is a fine example of a large Victorian residence. Built by Josiah Reynolds Neave, it became the Cottage Hospital in 1948 but is now a private nursing home.

156. Ernest Westlake, here photographed at the age of about eight in 1863, was to become a Fellow of the Geological Society and of the Royal Anthropological Institute. He was born at Southampton House in Horseport, Fordingbridge (a fact marked today by a blue plaque). He purchased Sandy Balls Estate in 1919 as a campsite for the Order of Woodcraft Chivalry and the Forest School, both of which he founded (see plates 22, 23 and 105).

157. The three Thompson brothers, Samuel, Edward and John, pictured c.1865. Samuel (on the right) was the owner of East Mills, where his company manufactured canvas. He died on 8 June 1867, aged 74 years. His firm continued at premises in Back Street (now West Street) until the Second World War. His son Henry was a farmer at Avonside near East Mill.

158. James Coventry of Burgate House was an enthusiastic amateur photographer in the 1890s and early 1900s. Many of his very accomplished compositions are featured in this volume. He appears to have taken around six thousand photographs, but only about three hundred of his 4in. by 3in. glass negatives are known to survive.

159. Mr. and Mrs. Coventry standing on the lawn in front of Burgate House. Its external features are early 19th-century Gothic in style, built onto an older house. It was the family home of the Coventrys from the 18th century until 1939 when the estate was split up. Today it is the headquarters of the Game Conservancy.

160.   Mr. and Mrs. Coventry with their family, either at Burgate House or at Burgate Cottage, *c*.1895. This provides a good example of how photographs can be dated from fashions—the elaborately trimmed hats were fashionable in the 1880s and 1890s, whilst tightly fitting blouse sleeves, puffed at the shoulder, were worn only after 1895.

161.   A group of four ladies, members of the Coventry family and friends, taking part in a children's game of Ring o' Roses—possibly a birthday party for one of the Coventry girls. In the background is an Aunt Sally figure. This is thought to be on the lawn of Burgate Cottage, now Burgate Court.

162.   Mrs. Coventry in a donkey cart at the front door of Burgate House. Standing by the donkey is Lady Adelaide Henrietta Goff of Hale House.

163. Hale House was rebuilt by Thomas Archer, Groom Porter to Queen Anne, in 1715, shortly after he purchased the estate. He also laid out the present park, including the fine lime avenue shown here. Archer was an accomplished architect of his day with numerous other renowned works to his credit, notably St Philip's in Birmingham (now the cathedral) and St Paul's in Deptford.

164. Lady Adelaide Goff of Hale House, well wrapped up against the winter cold, at the foot of the path leading to Hale church. The church is another example of Thomas Archer's architectural work. The medieval nave was kept but the classical style chancel and transepts were of his design in 1715.

165.   The Hulse family on the croquet lawn on the terrace of Breamore House, c.1867. Sir Edward Hulse, the 5th Baronet, is lying on the grass. Breamore House has been the home of the Hulse family since 1748.

166.   The Wilton hounds have met at Breamore for many years, usually during November and on Boxing Days, when the horses and hounds were followed on foot by many of the younger villagers. The future of hunting may be in doubt in the 1990s, but generations of country folk, here as elsewhere, have seen the chase as part of a traditional way of life.

167. West Park House was apparently constructed by Rev. Durnford of Rockbourne in 1720, but enlarged by General Sir Eyre Coote after his purchase of the estate in 1762. Its lands consisted largely of the old medieval deer-parks of Rockbourne and Damerham. The house fell into disrepair during the Second World War and was demolished in 1948.

168. General Sir Eyre Coote was a celebrated British officer, one of those responsible for the establishment of the Empire. He died in India in 1784 and his body was brought back to Rockbourne for burial. His sister arranged for this monument at West Park to be erected in his memory in 1827. Following restoration, it is now open to the public upon request.

169. The manor of Sandleheath is first mentioned in the 13th century and since then has often been connected with the nearby manor of Burgate. Sandle Manor was rebuilt by the Hulses of Breamore at the turn of the century, although its original Tudor style was retained. For many years now, the house has been occupied by Sandle Manor Preparatory School.

Farming

170.   Charles Mannell (leaning on a wheel) operated this threshing machine for 25 years. With him, beyond the fence, are Bill Lawes, Sam Gird and four farm workers. The Stuckton Iron Works had a long history of agricultural engineering. Here, in about 1920, Messrs. Armfield's were operating one of their own machines on contract work.

171. William Witt (in doorway) and Harry Read unloading sacks of grain from the barn over the cart-shed at Topp's Farm, Breamore, *c*.1925. The farm took its name from an early 18th-century tenant.

172. A team of ladies picking strawberries at Home Farm, Blissford, for the Witt family on a pleasant but cloudy early summer's day in 1930. The chip baskets of strawberries were sent to London by train or hawked around the local villages. Clearly visible in the background is Chilly Hill, part of the open heathland of the New Forest.

173. The strawberry pickers from the above photo with the results of their labours: over 270 full chip baskets. Left to right: Mrs. Witt, Mrs. Elliott, Mrs. Marlow, Mrs. Hayward, the three Clarke sisters of Bickton, Emily Chilcott, Miss Gilbert, Mrs. Blandford, Miss F. Gilbert. The dogs are 'White Jim' and 'Jack'.

174. John Wort of Stuckton (1864-1948), pauses from his labours for a rest on his pitchfork during haymaking at Hollwell Marsh near East Mill. The marsh was part of the manor of Nether Burgate and many tenants from the Stuckton area had held haymaking rights in it for centuries.

175. Percy Ponting was originally employed as a dairyman at Hale by the Goff family, but in about 1915 he took over a smallholding at Breamore, bought a few cows of his own, and set up in business. Over a period of 60 years, he and his son, Ernest, pastured their cows on Breamore Marsh and delivered milk to cottages around the village. This and the next six photographs give a picture of life on this smallholding from the 1930s to the 1950s.

176. Extracting mangolds (mangle-wurzles to some) from a straw covered clamp in which the crop was stored to protect it from frost. Mangolds were used as winter cattle feed. 'Nipper', the dog, is enjoying the view from the top of the clamp!

177. Geese grazing by their coop at Long Pond, Breamore Marsh. For centuries Breamore tenants have each been able to pasture a gander, two geese and their goslings on the marsh, but usually only the adults were allowed to survive Christmas! There were no such grazing rights for freeholders or for the lord of the manor, the rector or the miller.

178. Eliza Ponting feeding her hens in the farmyard of the smallholding. The building behind her is a cow-shed used to house and milk seven cows, whilst the attached lean-to section is a pig-sty.

179. Percy posing with his gun under his arm and 'Nipper' at his feet, following a ratting expedition. He is holding one of several ferrets he always kept for rabbiting on the Breamore Estate.

180.   Ernest and Nellie Ponting (parents of one of the authors) with faithful horse 'Captain' arriving home with a load of hay in the 1950s. The wagon has travelled half a mile along the (almost deserted) main road from the water meadows. (Ernest also appears in plate 101 as a Morris dancer.) Ron Hobbs' wheelwrights-cum-undertakers workshop in the background was destroyed by fire in the 1970s, as was the thatched roof of the cottage adjoining, which is now tiled and known as 'Wheelwrights'.

181. By the 1950s, tractors were fast replacing cart-horses on local farms. Here, as late as 1959, Ernest Ponting is taking his horse and wagon through a wide ford known as Longwaters to fetch hay from the water meadows. The cart-horse was replaced by a Ferguson tractor in 1960. (At the time of writing the tractor was still operational!)

Bibliography

Fordingbridge and District Directory (various editions 1888-1940).
Hannen, Reginald, *The History of Fordingbridge and Neighbourhood* (1909).
Kelly's Directory of Hampshire (various editions, 1875-1931).
Light, A. & Ponting, G., *Tudor Fordingbridge* (1993).
Morley Hewitt, A. T., *The Story of Fordingbridge in Fact and Fancy* (1965).
Victoria County History of Hampshire and the Isle of Wight (1911).